PJ'S STILL HUNGRY!

Bil Keane

FAWCETT GOLD MEDAL • NEW YORK

A Fawcett Gold Medal Book
Published by Ballantine Books
Copyright © 1981, 1982 by The Register and Tribune Syndicate, Inc.
Copyright © 1986 by King Features Syndicate, Inc.

Library of Congress Catalog Card Number: 86-91191

ISBN 0-449-13044-4

Manufactured in the United States of America

First Ballantine Books Edition: December 1986

10 9 8 7 6 5 4 3 2 1

"PJ is in there all alone wastin' some
of his smiles."

"I'm taking Billy to the library, Dolly to the party, Jeffy to a shoe store and PJ to the doctor. Then I'm going to shop for a chauffeur's cap."

"Mommy, know what PJ did?"

"Is he getting heavier or is it just late in the day?"

"The only thing wrong with soccer is you don't
get to wear hats."

"Look! My new jeans have a belly button!"

"Boy, this dollar sure has been spent a lot."

"Can we reach out and touch Grandma?"

"Hearing that rain makes me feel friendly,
Mommy — as long as it can't get
into the house."

"Gary is lucky. He's got TWO rooms — one at
his mother's house and one at
his father's house."

"They're water towers. One's for hot, and the other's for cold."

"Wow! Somebody hit the jackpot on
this apple tree."

"Who crayoned your windows?"

"They're all asleep. Now we can finally have some time for ourselves."

"I'm very warm, Mommy. Can you turn down the volume on the 'lectric blanket?"

"Lunch is ready. Harvest the children."

"Mommy, remember the new sweater
I'm wearing?"

"What kind of sandwich did Grandma make you?"
"I don't know. I didn't look inside before I ate it!"

"It works! I can hear you very clearly."

"Mommy, what did I do last Thursday?"

"She sure has a lot of names — Patty, Pat,
Trish, Patsy, Patricia. . . ."

"Mommy's going to broom the front path."

"We don't have to say grace, Jeffy. Daddy is paying for this."

"You hafta look out through the peephole
before you open the door."

"I figured out a system for getting along with my mom. She tells me what to do and I do it."

"Mommy always says a little prayer when she
takes off her shoes. She says 'Thank God.' "

"It's their anniversity, that's why."

"Because."
"Because why?"
"Just because. That's why."

"I think it's raining 'cause I see dimples in the birdbath."

"It's the cafeteria menu for next week.
Thursday would be a good day to be sick."

"I don't feel so good, Mommy. Can you get the
thermostat and check me?"

"Do I hafta go to school today? I feel a little bit absent."

"Look! It's a concrete blender."

"I wish the air would stand still."

"I didn't do anything. PJ opened the closet
door and I was just standing here
wearin' my Halloween mask."

"Do I hafta go out with Jeffy? He keeps forgetting and saying 'April Fool!'"

"We could cover a lot more places if you'd
drive us over to Condo Park."

"You forgot to put some Halloween candy in
my lunch bag so I had to borrow
some from Max."

"Mommy's cleanin' the bathroom. Are you the company we're 'specting?"

"Which channel do you turn on to make a milk shake?"

"It's lucky for John McEnroe that mommy isn't the umpire."

"I've got a marshmallow iceberg in my chocolate."

"AM means morning and FM means afternoon."

"Stop that crying or I'll give you something to cry about."

"What is it?"

"It's a smoke alarm. It lets mommy know if anybody's smoking."

"I think he's tryin' to remember where he put his clothes."

"Billy will be right out — as soon as he finds his other shoe."

"One more guess, Mommy, then if you're still
wrong I'll have to tell you what it is."

"Not now, Dolly."
"Well, will you do it as now as you can?"

"I don't like winter 'cause there's never any daytime left over after dinner."

"I don't want to see anything that has children in it."

"He's totaling aluminum cans."

"Why do they call milk 'milk'?"
"Because it's white."

"How 'bout a little one-on-one?"

"Let's play Supreme Court. You be the old guys
and I'll be Sandra Day O'Connor."

"It's the Mormon Tavernapple Choir."

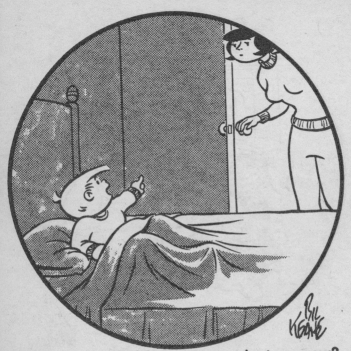

"Would you wake me up at six tomorrow?
That's when the cartoons start on TV."

"Why don't cards have any princesses?"

"Daddy said there's no such thing as a bogyman. Why do we need a burglar alarm?"

"Will the new alarm system put Sam and Barfy out of a job?"

"We forgot to turn off the alarm when we came in!"

"Will we turn off the burglar alarm on Christmas Eve so Santa won't set it off?"

"Everything's all right. It's just the burglar alarm sounding off by mistake again."

"Goldilocks would have been out of luck if the
Three Bears had had a burglar alarm."

"You better grow some more, Mommy. I'm gaining on you."

"The first rule of tooth care is never let anybody shove you when you're at the drinking fountain."

"I'm not dreamin' of a white Christmas 'cause I
think I'm getting roller skates."

"Can we go on that ride, Mommy?"

"I don't think he could remember my name. He called me sweetheart."

"We're gonna have REAL people at our
Christmas play. Not just parents."

"If you get caught under that mistletoe you
hafta get kissed."

"Stop it, P.J. Don't you know this is the season to be jolly?"

"Christmas seals are for envelopes,
not refrigerators."

"Bells on cocktails ring. . . ."

"Look! There's a porthole for George Washington to look through."

"New Year's Eve is for grownups."   "But Christmas is for kids!"

"Do we have a credit card for this store?"

"PJ took the tags off all the boxes!"

> The children were nestled
> all snug in their beds,
> While visions of sugarplums
> danced through their heads;

"What are sugarplums, Mommy?"

"This is the best Christmas I've ever had!"

"Why did Santa make this cane so short?"

"Billy gave it to me for Christmas. I don't think
it's a real diamond."

"Why don't we hafta write thank you letters to
Santa Claus?"

"When I snap my fingers it only makes a blank sound."

"What part of the fish do we get fish sticks from?"

"I'd rather watch TV with you, Grandma. All
Daddy watches is football games."

"Couldn't we give it a good drink of water and
leave it up for a couple more days?"

"Mommy wants her card table this instant!"

"In the olden days people were named after their jobs, like Mr. Baker, Mr. Taylor, Mr. Carpenter. . . ."

"What about Mr. Bombeck?"

"You're not to dribble that indoors anymore!"

"There's a light in there so the cookies can see."

"I wish they'd get to a commercial pretty soon
so I could go to the bathroom."

"You should have been with us, Daddy! Mommy
made the car spin around!"

"Why do all my stories have animals in them?"

"That's a neat badge, Mommy."

"I like crayons better. They don't dribble."

"Go back and close the door, young man.
We're not trying to heat the whole
neighborhood! Right, Mommy?"

"But he hit me back first!"

"Mommy, the fog is comin' out of the pea soup!"

"Could you play 'The Farmer in the Deli?'"

"Those are little bits of shell, Jeffy — not egg bones."

"Grandma, if you're going to buy me a surprise, can I pick it out?"

"Oops! I played the wrong number."

"Shall I give it a whack like mommy
always does?"

"A bread and butter note? Don't you hafta
thank them for the rest of the dinner?"

"Spring doesn't come till they run out of snow."

"How could they hang pictures in tepees?"

"I told Dolly my secret, Mommy. Make her tell me hers!"

"Only half of Jeffy's prayers count. He's
kneeling on one knee."

"Jack Spratt was on the Pritikin diet."

"Do angels lay eggs?"

"I'm tired, too, and nobody is carrying ME."

"Mommy! Billy said
a bad word."

"I didn't mean to. It
was a misprint."

"Why does she keep sayin', 'There you go, there you go'?"

"Is he going to do the dishes?"

"Ouch, Daddy! Your face needs a haircut!"

"I need a shirt with no buttons. Billy and I are
gonna have a race gettin' dressed."

"I winned the gettin'-dressed race!"

"I'm still reading it! When I've finished, THEN it can go to the Boy Scouts."

"Cupids are fat babies with no clothes on.
Angels wear white bathrobes
and circle hats."

"Is that the same old tantrum or are you
working on a new one?"

"Look! Daddy's walkin' his soap."

"See? They're all twins."

"He IS saying goodbye, Grandma, but he's just waving."